More Truths About
DOG PEOPLE

ISBN: 978-1-68088-559-0

and Blue Mountain Press are registered in U.S. Patent and Trademark Office. Certain trademarks are used under license.

Printed in China.
First Printing: 2025

This book is printed on recycled paper.

This book is printed on paper that has been specially produced to be acid free (neutral pH) and contains no groundwood or unbleached pulp. It conforms with the requirements of the American National Standards Institute, Inc., so as to ensure that this book will last and be enjoyed by future generations.

Blue Mountain Arts, Inc.
P.O. Box 4549, Boulder, Colorado 80306

More Truths About DOG PEOPLE

Jo Renfro

Blue Mountain Press™
Boulder, Colorado

Dog People
open their
hearts and
their homes.

C'mon, buddy! You're coming home with me.

Dog People start their days with a smile.

(Even if it's a little earlier than they'd like.)

All right, all right. Time to get up. I get it!

And they love a good, warm welcome!

Dog People realize that no one is perfect...

...and that sometimes life is messy.

(But they keep it in perspective.)

Dog People love to be outside...

What do you see? Oh wow! Good find! Baby birds!

...in every season...

...and all kinds of weather, because they know that attitude shapes the experience.

Dog People know that you're never too old to have fun.

But they also
appreciate
a good nap.

Dog People
are there for
their friends...

I'm home, bud! Let's get outside and go for a walk!
...and make spending time with them a priority.

ARF
ARF
ARF
ARF
ARF
ARF

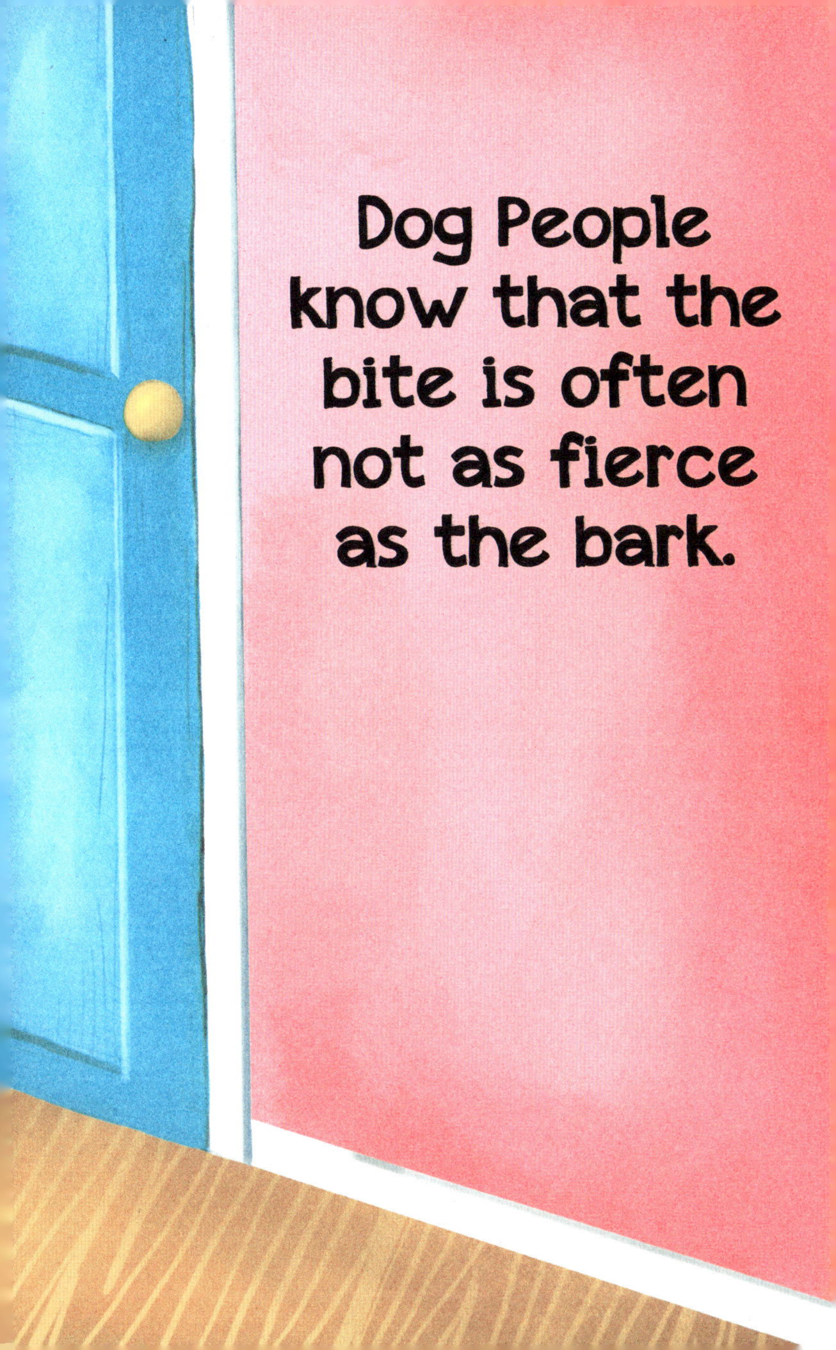

Dog People know that the bite is often not as fierce as the bark.

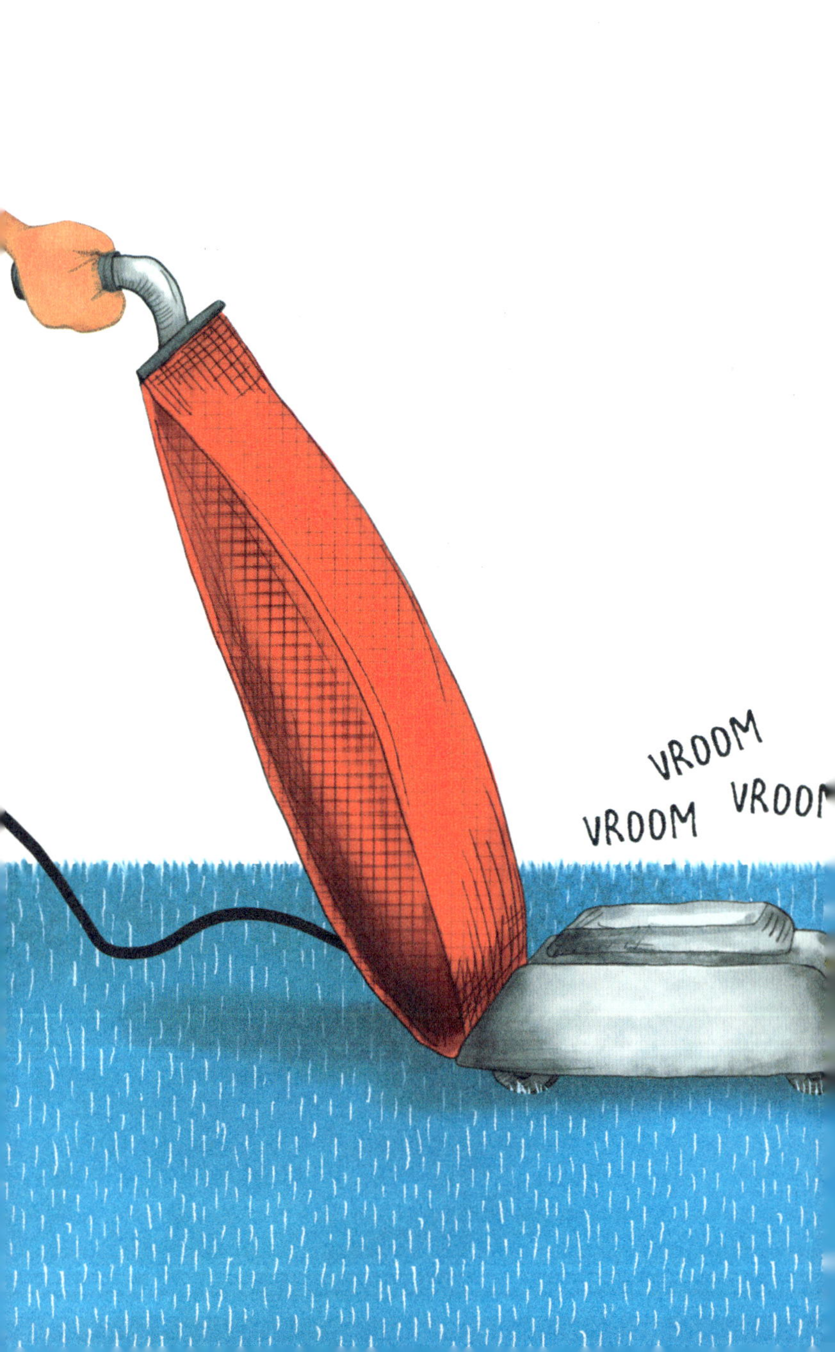
VROOM
VROOM
VROOM

And they believe it's important to face your fears.

Who wants a TREAT?

They understand the persuasive power of food...

...and the awesome power of a few kind words.

Aw! Look how cute!
Which one?
ALL of them!

Dog People love dogs of every shape, size, and color.

(How boring would life be if everyone looked the same?!)

Dog People
are soooo
lucky,
because
they get to
hang out
with dogs...

and
dogs
are the

BEST!

About the Author

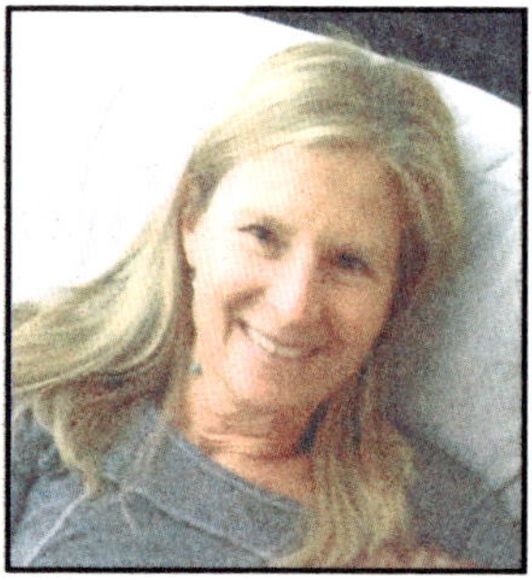

Jo Renfro is a freelance writer and illustrator with a passion for mixing color, pattern, and whimsy in her somewhat quirky, often amusing, and always upbeat work.

She enjoys using her sense of humor developed from raising three kids, several dogs, numerous cats, and a potbellied pig named Matilda to create pieces that are lightheartedly inspirational.

Her love of the outdoors, animals, and her amazing kids is often reflected in her work.

A lifelong Kansan, she recently moved to Colorado to be close to the mountains, which still take her breath away every single day.